PRAYER & STUDY GUIDE

The Power of
PRAYING®
THROUGH
Fear

STORMIE
OMARTIAN

HARVEST HOUSE PUBLISHERS
EUGENE, OREGON

All Scripture quotations are taken from the New King James Version®. Copyright © 1982 by Thomas Nelson, Inc. Used by permission. All rights reserved.

Cover by Bryce Williamson

Cover Image © axllll /iStock

Back cover author photo © Michael Gomez Photography

THE POWER OF PRAYING is a registered trademark of The Hawkins Children's LLC. Harvest House Publishers, Inc., is the exclusive licensee of the federally registered trademark THE POWER OF PRAYING.

Italics in quoted Scriptures indicates emphasis added by the author.

THE POWER OF PRAYING® THROUGH FEAR PRAYER AND STUDY GUIDE
Copyright © 2017 Stormie Omartian
Published by Harvest House Publishers
Eugene, Oregon 97402
www.harvesthousepublishers.com

ISBN 978-0-7369-6699-3 (pbk.)
ISBN 978-0-7369-6700-6 (eBook)

Printed in the United States of America

17 18 19 20 21 22 23 24 25 / BP-CD / 10 9 8 7 6 5 4 3 2 1

This book belongs to

_____

Please do not read beyond this page
without permission of the person named above.

A supplemental workbook to
The Power of Praying® Through Fear
by Stormie Omartian

Contents

What You Should Know Before You Begin

Welcome to this biblical study about what fear can do to you, what you fear most, and what the Bible says about fear and how to deal with it in the most positive way.

What You Need in Order to Begin

This *Prayer and Study Guide* is divided into a ten-week plan for personal or group study. You can also study two chapters a week if you would like a shorter five- to six-week study. Or you can do this study alone or with a prayer partner at your own pace.

You will need to have the book *The Power of Praying Through Fear* (it will be referred to as "the book" within each week's questions and directions). You must also have a Bible in which you are not hesitant to underline or write. All Bible quotes in the book (except for one in the New International Version) and this *Prayer and Study Guide* are from the New King James Version. But you can use whatever translation you feel most comfortable reading. You may also need a notebook or journal in which you can write some of the answers to these questions when you feel you have more to say than where you have room to write here. If you have that handy, you won't have to go looking for one when you are inspired to write more.

This *Prayer and Study Guide* is designed to give you practical tools to use whenever you feel fear encroaching upon your life. You will learn what to deliberately *think, say,* and *pray* when you have fear about anything, and also what you can do in response to it. You will be more prepared to help others handle their own fear.

As you respond to the questions and suggestions in each chapter, be completely honest because no one will be reading your answers. You do not have to share what you have written unless you want to do so.

When Doing This Study in a Group

If you are doing this *Prayer and Study Guide* in a group, read the chapter or chapters in the book that have been assigned for that week and then answer the corresponding questions for that chapter. At your next meeting, the leader will bring the group together and go over each question, and you can share any insights God has given you as you feel comfortable doing so. Even if you don't want to share personal information, you can share what God has shown you in prayer or through His Word. If you do feel like sharing insight with the group, you will find that it might not only be liberating for you to offer it, but also good for others to hear it.

If you do not have a group or are not able to start one yourself, don't forget that Jesus said where *"two or more are gathered"* in His name, He is there (Matthew 18:20). If you have a friend who wants to do this book with you and pray together, there is an exponential increase in the power of your prayers when you join in unity of purpose and faith to pray with that person.

All this doesn't mean God is not present in power when you do this study by yourself. The Bible says that "one can chase a thousand, and two put ten thousand to flight" (Deuteronomy 32:30). In fact, the tools in this book are designed to be used when you are alone and feeling fearful for whatever reason. Fear creeps up on us most often when we are alone.

When the section of Scripture you are being asked to read is lengthy, and you don't want to underline the entire text, just

WEEK ONE

Read the Introduction: "Say What?" and
Chapter 1: "What Can Fear Do to Us?"
in *The Power of Praying Through Fear*

1. Write out a prayer asking God to give you a new perspective on your life and on His plans for you. Ask Him for a deeper relationship with Him than you have ever experienced before. Everyone needs that.

_____

_____

_____

_____

We all have fear of some kind. List below all the things that cause you to have fear. Designate what frightens you most.

_____

_____

_____

_____

2. Read 2 Timothy 1:7 and underline it in your Bible. Put a star
    next to it. Write out that verse below, substituting the word "me"
    in place of the word "us."

    _____

    _____

    _____

    In light of this verse, what will you never receive from God?

    _____

    In light of this verse, what three gifts has God given you to
    combat your fears?

    1. _____

    2. _____

    3. _____

    Do you feel you have an abundance of those three gifts from
    God in your life? Write out your answer as a prayer. (For exam-
    ple, "Lord, I sense Your love for me, but I often feel weak in the
    face of my greatest fears. I need to sense Your power working
    in me and through me...")

    _____

    _____

    _____

    _____

3. Do you have any fear that affects your mind or emotions in a way that limits your life by taking away your joy, energy, confidence, or strength? If so, describe that.

_____

_____

_____

_____

Do you have fears that have been with you a long time? If so, how long? Describe those and what you believe has caused them.

_____

_____

_____

_____

_____

Write out a prayer asking God to show you anything that has happened in your past—even as recently as yesterday—that has caused you to have fear now that is damaging to your peace of mind and possibly your health.

_____

_____

_____

_____

Are any of your fears coming from what is going on in your mind or emotions? Describe what they are and why you think you have them.

_____

_____

_____

_____

4. Which of the following words would you use to describe your reaction to your greatest fears right now? ("I feel threatened, panicked, and incapacitated. I have feelings of insecurity, anxiety, or agitation...") What other words would you use to describe your reaction?

_____

_____

_____

_____

Do you have fear that in any way affects your physical body? (For example, "I have headaches. I am losing sleep. I often feel nervous and threatened. I am depressed. I am worried. I feel fear that is affecting my health and sense of well-being.") Write out your answer as a prayer telling God how you feel. Ask Him to set you free from those fears, and thank Him that He has given you what you need to combat fear and live in peace.

_____

_____

_____

_____

_____

5. Read John 8:31-32 and underline these verses in your Bible. In light of these words that Jesus said, what can set you free from fear?

    _____

    _____

    _____

    Write out a prayer asking God to continue to show you the truth in His Word that will set you free from fear.

    _____

    _____

    _____

    _____

6. We all have "What if?" fears that cause us to be afraid about things that *could* happen in the future, possibly as early as today. You may have a legitimate basis for those fears, or they may not even be relevant to your situation right now. List below all the "What if?" fears you can think of that you have, and beside each one write whether or not you believe the fear is justified. (Everyone has them, so don't hesitate to write them down. It helps to reduce their power.)

    _____

    _____

    _____

Write out a prayer bringing all these "What if this happens" type of thoughts before God. List each one specifically, and ask God to give you insight and comfort about them. Ask Him to take these fearful thoughts away and to tell you what, if anything, you can do about them.

_____

_____

_____

_____

_____

_____

7. Read 1 Thessalonians 5:14 and underline it in your Bible. It's not necessarily what we fear, but what we allow to overtake us that causes problems. Praying about everything that makes us afraid is a giant step to getting free of those fears. In light of this Scripture, what else are we to do?

_____

_____

_____

_____

_____

_____

8. Fear includes dread. Describe what you dread in your life. What do you dread that could possibly be ahead of you?

    _____

    _____

    _____

    _____

    Write out a prayer asking God to either take away what you are dreading or take away your feelings of dread. Ask Him to give you His peace and assurance that He will always be with you.

    _____

    _____

    _____

    _____

9. Look up the following Scriptures and underline them in your Bible. Beneath each one, tell what the people involved were instructed to do.

    Exodus 14:13

    _____

    _____

    _____

Joshua 10:25

_____

_____

_____

Deuteronomy 31:6

_____

_____

_____

Joshua 1:9

_____

_____

_____

Luke 8:50

_____

_____

_____

In light of the Scriptures above, what should you do when you feel fear?

_____

_____

_____

Read the following Scriptures and underline them in your Bible. Beneath each one, write out what that verse speaks to you personally and how it comforts or encourages you.

Psalm 27:1

_____

_____

_____

Isaiah 35:4

_____

_____

_____

Psalm 42:5

_____

_____

_____

Psalm 27:14

_____

_____

_____

10. Pray the prayer at the end of chapter 1 on page 33 in the book. Add any specifics of your life that you want to pray about concerning longtime fears you have had. Jot them down here to remind you to pray again about them.

_____

_____

_____

_____

_____

WEEK TWO

Read Chapter 2: "What Do We Fear Most?"
in *The Power of Praying Through Fear*

1. Read Psalm 34:4 and underline it in your Bible. What do you
   need to do with regard to your fear? And what will He do?

   _____

   _____

   _____

   _____

   Write out a prayer telling God about your greatest fears and ask
   Him to deliver you from the grip they have on you.

   _____

   _____

   _____

   _____

2. Read the following Scriptures and underline them in your Bible.
   Beneath each of these verses, tell what takes away darkness and
   what hope you have when you go through dark times.

John 8:12

_____

_____

_____

John 12:46

_____

_____

_____

Matthew 4:16

_____

_____

_____

Luke 11:35-36

_____

_____

_____

Is there a dark and frightening place in your mind, memory, or experience that you want to have enlightened and eliminated from your life? Describe that in a prayer, asking Him to set you free from this darkness so you can live fully in His light.

_____

_____

_____

Sometimes going back to examine a dark place in your memory, but with a new perspective, lessens the fear. That doesn't mean you have to revisit a frightening person, place, or situation again, but just going back to revisit that in your mind—with God being with you and showing you what is true now—can make a difference. Write out a prayer asking God to be with you and help you do that. If you need a friend, prayer partner, or counselor to pray with you at the same time, don't hesitate to ask someone.

_____

_____

_____

_____

3. Read 1 John 4:18 and underline it in your Bible. The perfect love this verse is talking about is the love of God. What can fear do to us, and what can get rid of it?

_____

_____

_____

_____

4. Read Psalms 49:5 and 50:14-15 and underline these verses in your Bible. Does the fear of evil people and their evil acts frighten you? What do you fear most concerning that?

_____

_____

_____

_____

Write out a prayer asking God to protect you and your loved ones from evil people and their evil works. Thank Him that He has the power to do that.

_____

_____

_____

_____

5. Read the following verses and underline them in your Bible. Beneath each one, write what that verse means for you personally with regard to your fears.

Psalm 18:19

_____

_____

_____

John 6:37

_____

_____

_____

Matthew 10:28-31

_____

_____

_____

6. Have you ever had a fear of being insignificant, unimportant, or invisible to other people? If so, describe that feeling and what you think has caused you to feel that way. If not, why do you think you have never felt that way?

_____

_____

_____

_____

Read Psalm 18:19 again. How does God think of you?

_____

_____

_____

7. Have you ever felt the fear of being rejected or criticized by other people? Have you been rejected in your past, and has it caused you to fear rejection now? Have you experienced rejection or harsh criticism that has made you afraid? If so, what was it that caused you to feel this way? Write out your answer as a prayer asking God to take away the pain of that horrible memory. (For example, "Lord, ever since I was made fun of in front of people, it has caused me to feel anxious around others now and...")

_____

_____

_____

_____

Read Proverbs 29:25 and Isaiah 51:7-8 and underline these verses in your Bible. In light of these Scriptures, what is the answer to any fear of rejection or criticism you may have?

_____

_____

_____

_____

8. Do you ever have fear when speaking in front of people—from a small group of friends to a larger group of people? What are you afraid of most?

_____

_____

_____

_____

Read 1 Corinthians 2:4-5 and underline these verses in your Bible. In this description by Paul, what did he think of and desire most when speaking to people?

_____

_____

_____

_____

Write out the verses above in a prayer for yourself. (For example, "Lord, I am afraid that when I speak, I won't speak well enough or won't say anything important enough. Help me to speak by the power and enablement of...")

_____

_____

_____

_____

Read Isaiah 54:4 and underline it in your Bible. What does this verse speak to you about being shamed or disgraced, for whatever reason?

_____

_____

_____

_____

What is the exact thought that runs through your mind when you are feeling fear about this issue? Write it out as a prayer. (For example, "Lord, whenever I think of getting up to speak in front of people, I panic and am afraid that my mind will go blank and...")

_____

_____

_____

_____

Read Psalm 31:1 and Hebrews 13:6 and underline these verses in your Bible. Write out the thoughts in them as a prayer you can pray whenever you have to speak in front of anyone. (For example, "Lord, whenever I have to speak in front of anyone, help me to put my trust in...")

_____

_____

_____

_____

_____

9. There is so much to be afraid of with regard to what is going on in the world around us. Everyone fears the violence, destruction, pain, and suffering that is being caused by evil people. Pray a covering of protection over every place you or your family go at any time, without exception. Write out a prayer listing the places and people you want to see protected and made safe. (For example, "Lord, I pray for my safety and the safety of my family at the school, the mall, the baseball field, the concert hall, the movie theater, the restaurant...") Be specific.

_____

_____

_____

_____

_____

_____

Write out a prayer for your government—local and national—that God will raise up godly and wise people who make wise decisions. Ask Him to expose and weed out all corruption, godlessness, and stupidity. Thank Him that all things are possible with Him.

_____

_____

_____

_____

_____

_____

Read Psalm 18:18 and underline it in your Bible. Write out this verse as a prayer thanking God that He is your support.

_____

_____

_____

_____

10. Pray the prayer at the end of chapter 2 on page 57 in the book. Add any concerns you may have that are specific to your life. Jot them below so you will remember to pray for them again.

_____

_____

_____

_____

_____

WEEK THREE

Read Chapter 3: "What Does the Bible Say About Fear?"
in *The Power of Praying Through Fear*

1. Read the following Scriptures and underline them in your Bible. Beneath each one, tell if you relate to any of the feelings of fear David had. What did David do or *want* to do?

   Psalm 3:1-6

   _____

   _____

   _____

   Psalm 4:1

   _____

   _____

   _____

   Psalm 55:5-7

   _____

   _____

   _____

Read the following Scriptures, and beneath each one, write what David did in the face of fear.

Psalm 55:16-18

_____

_____

_____

Psalm 55:22

_____

_____

_____

2. Read the following Scriptures and underline them in your Bible. Beneath each one, write what Jesus is saying to the people around Him and what hope He gives them.

Matthew 8:26

_____

_____

_____

Matthew 10:26

_____

_____

_____

Luke 12:32

_____

_____

_____

3. Read Psalm 4:6-7 and underline these verses in your Bible. Who is the one you can rely on to do good to you? What will He do?

_____

_____

_____

Write out a prayer thanking God for His goodness that is always extended toward you. Be specific about examples of His goodness in your life.

_____

_____

_____

_____

4. Read the story of Elisha and his servant in 2 Kings 6:8-23 and underline verses 16-17. Keep in mind that Elisha always walked closely with God. What did Elisha tell his servant when he saw they were surrounded by their enemy? (verse 16)

_____

_____

_____

_____

What did Elisha pray for his servant, and how did God answer that prayer? (verse 17)

_____

_____

_____

_____

What did Elisha pray that God would do to his enemy? (verse 18)

_____

_____

_____

_____

What did Elisha do to mislead the enemy? (verses 19-23)

_____

_____

_____

_____

Read Romans 8:31 and underline it in your Bible. What does this verse mean to you in light of your fears? Write out your answer as a prayer. (For example, "Lord, in light of my fear of being attacked by people, I am comforted because I see that...") Ask God to help you see things from His perspective.

_____

_____

_____

5. Do you ever feel overwhelmed by the opposition and struggle facing you? (For example, sickness in your family, financial stress, relationship strains, dangerous places you might be working in, sudden violence, etc.) Write out a prayer describing what concerns you most with regard to doing what you need to do. Ask Him to protect you in the face of opposition.

_____

_____

_____

_____

_____

_____

Read Zechariah 4:6-7. Describe how Zerubbabel would be able to do what he needed to do (which was to rebuild the holy temple). God told him it wouldn't be by the power and resources of men. How would it be accomplished?

_____

_____

_____

_____

What was Zerubbabel required to speak to his mountain of opposition? (verse 7)

_____

_____

_____

In light of these two verses, what should you rely on in order to get beyond the opposition you face in your life?

_____

_____

_____

Write out a prayer asking God to help you rely on the power of His Spirit and His grace when facing your fears and any opposition.

_____

_____

_____

_____

Read 1 Chronicles 28:20 and underline it in your Bible. What did King David instruct his son Solomon to do when he was called by God to build the temple?

_____

_____

_____

_____

6. Read the following Scriptures and underline them in your Bible. Beneath each one, write the words of Jesus in your own words, beginning with either "I believe..." or "Help me to believe..." depending on whether you believe these words of Jesus or you still have doubt.

John 3:3-6

_____

_____

_____

John 3:16

_____

_____

_____

John 3:17-18

_____

_____

_____

John 6:47

_____

_____

_____

John 10:9

_____

_____

_____

John 6:65

_____

_____

_____

John 14:1

_____

_____

_____

Write out a prayer below thanking God for all He has promised to you in the Scriptures above. (For example, "Thank You, Lord, that because I have received You and I am born again, I can now see Your kingdom...")

_____

_____

_____

_____

_____

_____

7. Read the following Scriptures and underline them in your Bible. Beneath each one, write out a prayer of thanks to God for the benefits He has given you promised in that verse.

John 1:12

_____

_____

_____

Romans 8:9

_____

_____

_____

2 Corinthians 5:17

_____

_____

_____

John 3:36

_____

_____

_____

Romans 10:10

_____

_____

_____

8. Read the following Scriptures and underline them in your Bible. Beneath each one, write down why having faith in God and His Word is good.

Hebrews 11:1

_____

_____

_____

Hebrews 11:6

_____

_____

_____

Romans 14:23

_____

_____

_____

Matthew 17:20

_____

_____

_____

James 1:6

_____

_____

_____

9. God's Spirit in us proves that we have received Jesus and assures us that we have been adopted as one of His children. He is our heavenly Father. We have been freed from having to live in bondage to a spirit of fear and can now live in freedom from fear. Read the following Scriptures and underline them in your Bible. Beneath each one, write why it is important to be led by God's Spirit.

Romans 8:7-8

_____

_____

_____

John 7:38

_____

_____

_____

Romans 8:13-14

_____

_____

_____

Read the following Scriptures and underline them in your Bible. Beneath each one, write out how that verse reveals God's love for you.

John 4:18

_____

_____

_____

Isaiah 43:1

_____

_____

_____

Isaiah 41:10

_____

_____

_____

Romans 8:15

_____

_____

_____

Ephesians 3:16-19

_____

_____

_____

2 Timothy 2:19

_____

_____

_____

Nahum 1:7

_____

_____

_____

Write out a prayer thanking God that the more you are perfected in His love, the more your fears will fade. Thank Him specifically for what is mentioned in the Scriptures above that especially touched your heart.

_____

_____

_____

_____

_____

10. Pray the prayer at the end of chapter 3 on pages 74-75 in the book. Add your own specific requests and jot them below so you will remember to pray for them again.

_____

_____

_____

_____

_____

WEEK FOUR

Read Chapter 4: "What Is the Fear God *Allows* Us to Experience?"
in *The Power of Praying Through Fear*

1. Read the following Scriptures and underline them in your Bible. Beneath each one, write in your own words what God wants you to do and why it would be a good thing to do that whenever you feel afraid.

   James 4:8

   _____

   _____

   _____

   Hebrews 10:22

   _____

   _____

   _____

   Psalm 73:28

   _____

   _____

   _____

Fill in the blanks: (See the first full paragraph on page 79 in the book.) The kind of fear God *allows* will always _____ you _____ to _____ in _____ and _____ into His _____ for _____ and _____, and it helps you to _____ a _____ _____ of His _____ _____.

2. Read Psalm 19:7-14 and underline your favorite verses in this passage of Scripture in your Bible. In the following verses, how are the laws of God described, and what do they accomplish for us when we live by them?

Verse 7: The law of the Lord is described as

_____,

and what it does for us is

_____.

The testimony of the Lord is

_____,

and what it does is

_____.

Verse 8: The statutes of the Lord are

_____,

and what they do is

_____.

The commandment of the Lord is

_____,

and what it does for us is

_____.

Verse 9: The fear of the Lord is

_____,

and what it does is

_____.

The judgments of the Lord are

_____.

Verse 10: How are we supposed to think of God's commands and laws?

_____

_____

_____

Verse 11: How does God use them to our benefit?

_____

_____

_____

Verses 12-14: Can we always see our own sins or mistakes? How did David, who wrote this psalm, pray to God? Write out your answers as a prayer. (For example, "Lord, I recognize I do not always understand my own errors and sins, and I cannot presume that I do. So I ask You to...")

_____

_____

_____

_____

Read 1 Corinthians 8:2 and underline it in your Bible. What must we not assume?

_____

_____

In light of this Scripture and the verses from Psalm 19:7-14, why do you need to have the Word of God in your heart and mind?

_____

_____

_____

_____

_____

3. It's extremely important to pray about every fear you have. Take each one to God and ask Him for discernment regarding them. Do you have uncomfortable feelings about any person or situation that gives you a gut-level lack of peace or fear—even if you don't have hard evidence of imminent danger? Write out a prayer below telling God what you are sensing. Ask Him to show you if your suspicions are valid or not. He will give you

peace if they are not. Ask God to give you discernment about what you should do regarding those fears. (For example, "Lord, I'm concerned about where my daughter is working. I don't feel it's safe, and I fear something could happen to her when she leaves work after dark. Lead her to a safe workplace...")

_____

_____

_____

_____

_____

Read Matthew 18:20 and underline it in your Bible. Describe what this means to you with regard to praying with others about your concerns.

_____

_____

_____

_____

4. Have you ever had sudden fear, and it proved to be a warning sign from God that caused you to draw near to Him in prayer and ask for guidance? Have you ever had God put someone on your heart, and you felt fear for them? Do you have fear or extreme concern for yourself or someone right now? If you answered yes to any of those three questions, write out a prayer regarding that.

_____

_____

_____

_____

_____

Have you ever had a prompting from the Lord to change your plans or do something different than what you were going to do? Describe that in a prayer asking God to give you discernment every day and make you sensitive to His leading. (See "Don't Ignore Your God-Given Discernment" on pages 82-84 in the book.)

_____

_____

_____

_____

5. What are you afraid could happen to you, or your family, or friends, or in your community or town? Write out your answer as a prayer regarding what you fear. (For example, "Lord, I am afraid the violence I see happening in our town could come to my neighborhood. I pray You would protect our neighborhood and keep all evil from coming here. Let no weapon formed against us succeed...")

_____

_____

_____

_____

Write out a prayer covering every place you go or are concerned about. If you frequent a certain mall, church, theater, restaurant, or whatever, mention those specific places. Don't go anywhere without praying for the protection and will of God to reign there. Don't assume everything will be fine if you don't pray.

_____

_____

_____

_____

_____

Write out a prayer for your city and your country. If you see a news report or prediction that something bad is inevitable, pray to almighty God and ask Him to keep that from happening. Ask Him to do what others are predicting is impossible.

_____

_____

_____

_____

_____

Read Daniel 9:20-22 and underline these verses in your Bible. What was Daniel doing before the angel Gabriel appeared to him? (verse 20)

_____

_____

_____

_____

Read Daniel 10:2-14 and underline these verses in your Bible. How long did Daniel fast and pray before he received an answer from the Lord? (verses 2-3)

_____

_____

_____

_____

What did the angel tell Daniel? (verses 10-13)

_____

_____

_____

_____

In light of these Scriptures, how do you believe you are to pray about your own city and country? Write out your answer as a prayer. Keep in mind that our prayers must be ongoing because of the spiritual battle between good and evil in every country. Ask God to show you how to pray so you can be sure.

_____

_____

_____

_____

6. Read the following Scriptures and underline them in your Bible. Beneath each one, describe how the words of these Scriptures relate to your life. (For example, in John 15:8, "God is glorified when I bear good fruit in my life, and it shows I am a disciple of Christ...")

John 15:8

_____

_____

_____

Matthew 7:17

_____

_____

_____

John 15:1-2

_____

_____

_____

John 15:16

_____

_____

_____

7. Read Galatians 5:22-23 and underline these verses in your Bible.
    When we do not manifest the fruit of the Spirit in our lives, it
    shows we are not walking closely with God, and we can expe-
    rience unrest, anxiety, and fear. The first three fruit of the Spirit
    are _____, _____, and _____.
    Write out a prayer asking God to manifest these three charac-
    teristics of His nature in you. Thank Him for these gifts of His
    Spirit, and ask Him to show you whenever they are not percep-
    tible or strong enough in you for others to appreciate and glo-
    rify God because of them.

    _____

    _____

    _____

    _____

    _____

8. The second three fruit of the Spirit are _____,
    _____, and _____.
    Write out a prayer asking God to manifest those characteristics
    in your attitude. Ask Him to help you have an abundant crop so
    you can be that way at all times. With which one do you want
    the most help?

    _____

    _____

    _____

    _____

    _____

9. The last three fruit of the Spirit are _____,
   _____, and _____.
   These have to do with the way we all should live. They reflect
   our godly character and whether we are Spirit controlled or flesh
   controlled. Write out a prayer asking God to help you exhibit
   these characteristics at all times, and to show you where you
   need to improve.

   _____

   _____

   _____

   _____

   _____

10. Pray the prayer on page 97 at the end of chapter 4. Include any
    specifics that God brings to mind concerning your life. Jot them
    down below to remind you to pray about this again.

    _____

    _____

    _____

    _____

    _____

WEEK FIVE

Read Chapter 5: "What Is the Fear God *Wants* Us to Have?"
in *The Power of Praying Through Fear*

1. Read the first paragraph of this chapter and complete the sentences below.

    The only fear God wants us to have is _____
    _____

    The fear of God the Bible talks about is actually _____
    _____
    _____

    Have you ever experienced fear that was a good thing because
    it led you to turn to God, get away from danger, or pray for
    someone you felt God had put on your heart? Explain.

    _____
    _____
    _____
    _____

Read Jeremiah 32:40 and underline it in your Bible. What was the covenant God wanted to make with His people?

_____

_____

_____

_____

Read Proverbs 2:1-6 and underline these verses in your Bible. How do you find and understand the fear of God?

_____

_____

_____

_____

_____

2. Read Deuteronomy 10:12-13 and underline these verses in your Bible. After Moses was used by God to bring the Israelites out of slavery, and they were given the Ten Commandments and sent on their journey to the land God had promised to them, they were instructed to do five things. List them below.

    1. To fear

    _____

    2. To walk

    _____

3. To love

_____

4. To serve

_____

_____

5. To keep

_____

_____

Write out a prayer asking God to help you do the five things above.

_____

_____

_____

_____

Read Hebrews 11:7 and underline it in your Bible. What motivated Noah to build the ark?

_____

_____

_____

Read Deuteronomy 5:29 and underline it in your Bible. What does God want from us? What is the reward?

_____

_____

_____

_____

Read Deuteronomy 13:4 and underline it in your Bible. What does God want us to do?

_____

_____

_____

3. Read "The Benefits of Having the Fear of God" on pages 101-103 in the book. List the benefits below.

When we have the fear of God...

1. _____

2. _____

3. _____

4. _____

5. _____

6. _____

7. _____

8. _____

9. _____

10. _____

Write out a prayer asking God to help you always have a heart that reverences Him and thank Him for each of the ten blessings above that come as a result.

_____

_____

_____

_____

_____

_____

_____

4. Read "The Truth About God-Fearing People" on pages 103-106 in the book. List 15 things that are true of God-fearing people below.

People who fear God...

1. _____

2. _____

3. _____

4. _____

5. _____

6. _____

7. _____

8. _____

9. _____

10. _____

11. _____

12. _____

13. _____

14. _____

15. _____

Write out a prayer thanking God for each of these blessings to you as a God-fearing person. Ask Him to help you forever reverence Him in your heart so that these will always be true of you.

_____

_____

_____

_____

_____

_____

_____

_____

5. Read the following Scriptures and underline them in your Bible. Beneath each one, write down how the fear of God is revealed in us.

    Leviticus 25:17

    _____

    _____

    _____

Deuteronomy 8:6

_____

_____

_____

Leviticus 19:32

_____

_____

If we have the fear of God, we will...

Psalm 119:63

_____

_____

_____

Psalm 115:13

_____

_____

_____

6. Read Colossians 1:9-12 and underline these verses in your Bible. Why do we need to be filled with the knowledge of God's will and have wisdom and spiritual understanding?

_____

_____

_____

_____

_____

_____

Read Proverbs 3:13-18 and underline these verses in your Bible.
What is the advantage of having the wisdom of God given to
those of us who fear Him?

_____

_____

_____

_____

_____

Read Proverbs 1:33 and underline it in your Bible. What happens to those who listen to godly wisdom?

_____

_____

7. Read Proverbs 1:24-29 and underline these verses in your Bible.
    What happens to those who refuse to reverence God and don't
    have the fear of the Lord in them?

_____

_____

_____

_____

_____

_____

Read Proverbs 10:24 and underline it in your Bible. What happens to the wicked? What happens to those who fear God?

_____

_____

Read Proverbs 10:27 and underline it in your Bible. What happens to the wicked? What happens to those who fear God?

_____

_____

8. Read the following Scriptures and underline them in your Bible. Beneath each one, tell what the benefits of godly wisdom are. Read also, "The Benefits of Having Godly Wisdom" on pages 106-108 in the book.

Isaiah 33:6

_____

_____

_____

Proverbs 3:21-24

_____

_____

_____

Proverbs 4:5-9

_____

_____

_____

Read the following Scriptures and underline them in your Bible. Beneath each one, write down how we get godly wisdom and what will happen when we do that.

James 1:5

_____

_____

_____

Proverbs 2:6-7

_____

_____

_____

Proverbs 9:10

_____

_____

_____

Proverbs 3:21-24

_____

_____

_____

Proverbs 2:10-12

_____

_____

_____

9. Read 1 Corinthians 3:19-20 and underline these verses in your Bible. Describe worldly wisdom.

_____

_____

_____

Read "The Truth About Godly Wisdom Versus Worldly Wisdom" on pages 108-110 in the book. What is the difference between worldly wisdom and the wisdom that comes from God?

_____

_____

_____

_____

_____

Read 1 Corinthians 1:18-21 and 2:7-8 and underline these verses in your Bible. How is the wisdom of God brilliantly illustrated in Jesus' death and resurrection on the cross? (See pages 109-110 in the book.)

_____

_____

_____

_____

_____

Since you have received the Lord, how differently do you see things from the way you saw them before? How has the wisdom God has given you changed the way you make decisions or prioritize your life?

_____

_____

_____

_____

_____

Read Proverbs 10:25 and underline it in your Bible. What happens to the worldly compared to the godly?

_____

_____

_____

_____

10. Pray the prayer at the end of chapter 5 on page 111 in the book. Include specifics you also want to pray about. Jot them down here so you will remember to pray about them again.

_____

_____

_____

_____

_____

WEEK SIX

Read Chapter 6:
"What Must We *Think*, *Say*, and *Pray* When We Are Afraid?"
in *The Power of Praying Through Fear*

1. Read Matthew 21:22 and underline it in your Bible. What do these words of Jesus say to you about your own prayers? What do you need to do to receive answers to your prayers? Write out your answers as a prayer. (For example, "Lord Jesus, Your words about prayer tell me that...")

   _____

   _____

   _____

   _____

   Write out a prayer telling God about your greatest fear right now and ask Him to give you wisdom as to what to pray, and the faith you need to believe He will answer your prayers regarding that.

   _____

   _____

   _____

   _____

2. Read Acts 12:1-17 and underline key verses in your Bible. What was Herod's attitude toward believers? (verse 1)

_____

_____

What did Herod do to James? (verse 2)

_____

_____

Why did Herod arrest Peter? (verse 3)

_____

_____

How securely was Peter imprisoned? (verses 4 and 6)

_____

_____

_____

_____

What was happening with the believers while Peter was in prison? (verse 5)

_____

_____

What happened to Peter the night before Herod was going to bring him out of prison, probably for execution, while he slept chained to the two soldiers? (verses 7-9)

_____

_____

_____

_____

What happened after he passed the two guard posts and came to the big iron gate that led out of the prison? What did Peter realize? (verses 10-11)

_____

_____

_____

_____

What was happening with the people at Mary's house when Peter knocked at the gate? How did the people react when they heard Peter was there? (verses 12-15)

_____

_____

_____

_____

The people didn't believe God had answered their prayers, so they didn't open the door right away. (verse 16) Is there any fear you have that causes you to doubt that God will answer your prayer right away? Write out your answer as a prayer below, asking God to help you believe that all things are possible with Him.

_____

_____

_____

_____

3. Read Acts 16:16-34 and underline key verses in your Bible. Why were Paul and Silas thrown in prison? (verses 16-21)

_____

_____

_____

_____

What was done to Paul and Silas once the people rose up against them? (verses 22-24)

_____

_____

_____

_____

What were Paul and Silas doing at midnight, and what happened as a result of that? (verses 25-26)

_____

_____

_____

_____

What was the reaction of the jail keeper? What happened to him? What happened to his family? (verses 27-34)

_____

_____

_____

_____

What were Paul and Silas doing before the earthquake happened? They were worshiping God and praying. This was their most difficult situation, and it dramatically changed at that point. Write out a prayer describing your most difficult situation right now. Use words of worship and praise to God, thanking Him that He is more powerful and greater than anything you face. Thank Him for the miracles He can do, even when you see no way out of a situation. Thank Him for the chains that fall off you every time you worship Him.

_____

_____

_____

_____

_____

4. Read Romans 8:25-28 and underline verses 26 and 28 in your Bible. Sometimes we don't know what to pray. This could be because we have prayed about the same thing for so long we wonder if perhaps we are not praying the right way. Or we are so overwhelmed by what we are praying about that we don't know where to start or how to put it into words. Whatever the reason, the Holy Spirit will help us pray. He doesn't pray instead of us. He helps us pray effectively.

Do you see a connection between your prayers and things working out for good for those who love God and are called according to His purpose for their life? Can you think of an important situation in your life that you want to work out for good, but you sometimes fear it won't? Write out your answer as a prayer asking the Holy Spirit to help you to pray about this. Tell Him what you would like to see happen, but more than anything that you want His perfect will to be done.

_____

_____

_____

_____

_____

_____

5. Read Romans 12:1-2 and underline these verses in your Bible. What should we do every day? (verse 1)

_____

_____

What should we *not* do? (verse 2)

_____

_____

What happens when we do that?

_____

_____

Write out a prayer asking God to help you do the things He wants you to do and *not* do the things He doesn't want you to do. Ask Him to show you specifically where you are conforming to this world, and ask Him to give you a transformed mind.

_____

_____

_____

_____

_____

6. Read 1 John 4:15 and underline it in your Bible. When we speak the truth about God and His Word, Jesus becomes more real in our heart. The more we think about God's Word, and we speak His Word aloud boldly, and pray about the things that concern us, the weaker our fears grow. Write out a prayer asking God to help you tell someone what you know about Jesus and how He has changed your life.

_____

_____

_____

_____

The last section of this chapter is called "Twenty Things to *Think, Say,* and *Pray* When You Are Afraid." What are the first five truths about God (1-5) that you need to think about? Write out your answer as a prayer. (For example, "Thank You, Lord, that You are always with me, and You never leave me or forsake me. Thank You that You are always on my side...")

_____

_____

_____

_____

_____

Along with these first five truths are the Scriptures to back them up, and also a short prayer you can pray whenever you feel afraid. Write out in your own words one of these five Scriptures you want to memorize first to help you get rid of fear. (For example, "I want to remember that God is our refuge and strength, a very present help in trouble." Sometimes I feel I'm all alone when I'm going through troubled times, and that makes my fear greater." Then write out that Scripture.)

_____

_____

_____

_____

_____

7. What are the next five truths about God (6-10) that you need to think about? Write out your answer as a prayer. (For example, "Thank You, Lord, that any time I need help I can call Your name and You are with me...")

_____

_____

_____

_____

_____

Which of the five Scriptures in numbers 6-10 do you want to remember most right now and why? (For example, "I need to remember 'No weapon formed against you shall prosper...'")

_____

_____

_____

_____

_____

8. What are the next five truths about God (11-15) that you need to think about? Write out your answer as a prayer. (For example, "Lord, I'm grateful You have angels watching out for me...")

_____

_____

_____

_____

_____

9. What are the last five truths about God (16-20) that you need to think about? Write out your answer as a prayer. (For example, "Thank You, Lord, that You answer my prayers when I pray in Your name...")

_____

_____

_____

_____

_____

Which of the five Scriptures in numbers 16-20 do you want to remember most right now and why? (For example, "I want to remember Jesus' words that say 'Whatever you ask in My name...'")

_____

_____

_____

_____

Read Philippians 4:6-7 and underline these verses in your Bible. Instead of having fear and anxiety, what are you to do instead? What will happen when you do that?

_____

_____

_____

_____

10. Pray the prayer at the end of chapter 6 on page 126 in the book. Include specifics you also want to pray about. Jot them down here so you will remember to pray about them again later.

_____

_____

_____

_____

_____

WEEK SEVEN

Read Chapter 7: "What Should We *Do* When We Feel Fearful?"
in *The Power of Praying Through Fear*

1. Read number 1, "Bring Every Thought into Captivity," on
   page 132 in the book. Then read the following Scriptures and
   underline them in your Bible. Beneath each one, write what
   God wants you to do with regard to your mind. Write out your
   answer as a prayer. (For example, "Lord, help me refuse to listen to arguments against You and Your ways or anything that
   exalts itself against You, and instead bring...")

   2 Corinthians 10:4-5

   _____

   _____

   _____

   Romans 12:2

   _____

   _____

   _____

Ephesians 4:22-24

_____

_____

_____

Romans 8:5-6

_____

_____

_____

Do you have any upsetting thoughts that come to your mind frequently, and you want to be free of them? If so, write them out in a prayer below. (For example, "Lord, I have thoughts about terrible things that could happen, and they take away my peace and make me afraid. Take those thoughts from me and help me to refuse to entertain them...")

_____

_____

_____

_____

Say the Scriptures and pray the prayer out loud in "Bring Every Thought into Captivity." Add whatever else God has put on your heart to pray. Jot it down below to remind you.

_____

_____

_____

Read number 5, "Deliberately Focus Your Mind on Good Things," on page 134 in the book. Read Psalm 94:11 and underline it in your Bible. What does God know about your mind when it is not surrendered to Him?

_____

_____

_____

Read Philippians 4:8-9 and underline these verses in your Bible. Who we are and what we do are affected by what we think. Below are things God asks us to think about. Think of a thought you could have that fits each description and write it down below it. Doing this can help you have peace in place of fearful or negative thoughts that may come to your mind.

Think about *what is true.* (What is true from God's perspective?) For example, "It's always true that God loves me." Or "God's Word is always true, and one of my favorite verses is..."

_____

_____

_____

Think about *what is noble.* (What is an excellent or elevated thought?)

_____

_____

_____

Think about *what is just.* (What is reasonable, proper, and fair?)

_____

_____

_____

Think about *what is pure.* (What is clean and free from contamination of any kind?)

_____

_____

_____

Think about *what is lovely.* (What is beautiful or exquisite?)

_____

_____

_____

Think about *what is of good report.* (What is good news to you?)

_____

_____

_____

Think about *what is of virtue.* (What has moral excellence and is ethical?)

_____

_____

_____

Think about *what is praiseworthy.* (What is something you want to praise God for?)

_____

_____

_____

Write out a prayer asking God to help you fill your mind with thoughts about things that fall into the eight categories above. Ask Him to help you replace fear-filled and negative thoughts with peaceful and positive thoughts.

_____

_____

_____

_____

Say the Scripture and pray the prayer out loud in "Deliberately Focus Your Mind on Good Things." Below, jot down any specifics that come to mind that you want to pray about as well.

_____

_____

_____

_____

2. Read number 2, "Commit Everything You Do to the Lord," on pages 132-133 in the book. Then read the following Scriptures and underline them in your Bible. Answer the questions by writing them out in a prayer. (For example, "Lord, Your Word says that..." or "Help me to...")

Proverbs 16:3. What happens to your mind when you commit all you do to the Lord?

_____

_____

_____

_____

Colossians 3:23. What attitude are you supposed to have in everything you do?

_____

_____

_____

_____

Say the Scripture and pray the prayer out loud in "Commit Everything You Do to the Lord." Add whatever else God has put on your heart to pray. Jot it down below to remind you.

_____

_____

_____

_____

Read number 3, "Decide to Trust God and Not Your Fear," on page 133 in the book. Then read the following Scriptures and underline them in your Bible. Beneath each one, write down what the reward is for trusting God.

Psalm 37:3-4

_____

_____

_____

Psalm 34:7-8

_____

_____

_____

Psalm 32:10

_____

_____

_____

Say the Scripture and pray the prayer out loud in "Decide to Trust God and Not Your Fear." Write out a prayer asking God to help you trust *Him* more than your fear.

_____

_____

_____

_____

3. Read number 4, "Express Your Love for God with Praise and Worship," on pages 133-134 in the book. Then read the following Scriptures and underline them in your Bible. Beneath each one, write out what you need to do and what the reward is for doing that.

Psalm 34:1-4

_____

_____

_____

Psalm 34:17-22

_____

_____

_____

Psalm 100:4-5

_____

_____

_____

Psalm 103:1-5

_____

_____

_____

Say the Scripture and pray the prayer out loud in "Express Your Love to God with Praise and Worship." Add whatever else God has put on your heart to pray. Jot it below to remind you.

_____

_____

_____

Read number 10, "Show Your Love for God by Living His Way," on page 137 in the book. Then read the following Scriptures and underline them in your Bible. Beneath each one, write out what it says about how to show your love for God and what happens as a result of living His way.

John 14:21

_____

_____

_____

John 15:10-11

_____

_____

_____

John 15:14

_____

_____

_____

Psalm 119:142-143

_____

_____

_____

John 14:23

_____

_____

_____

Say the Scripture and pray the prayer out loud in "Show Your Love for God by Living His Way." Add whatever else God has put on your heart to pray. Jot it below to remind you.

_____

_____

_____

4. Read number 6, "Ask God if You Need to Confess Anything to Him," on pages 134-135 in the book. Then read the following Scriptures and underline them in your Bible. Beneath each one, write what it says about confessing our errors to God.

    Proverbs 28:13

_____

_____

_____

1 John 1:8-9

_____

_____

_____

1 John 3:21

_____

_____

_____

Psalm 38:17-18

_____

_____

_____

Psalm 32:5

_____

_____

_____

Say the Scripture and pray the prayer out loud in "Ask God if You Need to Confess Anything to Him." Add whatever else God has put on your heart to pray. Jot it below to remind you.

_____

_____

_____

Read number 18, "Forgive Others, and Make No Plans for Revenge," on pages 143-144 in the book. We all need to ask God to show us if we have any unforgiveness in us. Not forgiving someone is a sure way to stop receiving all God has for us. It will cause us to have anxiety and fear and put up a road block between us and God until we get rid of it.

Read Matthew 18:21-35 and underline key verses in your Bible. What happened when the wicked servant refused to forgive another person after he had been forgiven so much by his master? (see verses 32-35)

_____

_____

_____

_____

Read the following Scriptures and underline them in your Bible. Beneath each one, write what we should do and why.

Mark 11:25

_____

_____

_____

Ephesians 4:30-31

_____

_____

_____

Luke 17:3-4

_____

_____

_____

Romans 12:17-19

_____

_____

_____

Colossians 3:12-13

_____

_____

_____

Say the Scripture and pray the prayer out loud in "Forgive Others, and Make No Plans for Revenge." Add whatever else God has put on your heart to pray. Jot it below to remind you.

_____

_____

_____

5. Read number 7, "Be a Doer of the Word," on pages 135-136 in the book. Then read the following Scriptures and underline them in your Bible. Beneath each one, describe what it says to you about not just reading or hearing about God's laws, but

actually doing what the Word says and what happens when you do. (For example, "Lord, I know You require more of me than just hearing the law. You want me to...so I can...")

Romans 2:13

_____

_____

_____

James 1:25

_____

_____

_____

Say the Scripture and pray the prayer out loud in "Be a Doer of the Word." Add whatever else God has put on your heart to pray. Jot it below to remind you.

_____

_____

_____

Read number 9, "Read God's Word Daily Until You Feel Relief from Fear," on page 136 in the book. I don't believe it's possible to be free of fear without God's Word in our heart. Part of spending time with God is being in His Word. That's because He meets you there when you seek His presence.

Read Isaiah 41:10. In light of this verse, what does God's presence accomplish in your life? Write out your answer as a prayer and ask Him to set you free from fear every time you read His Word. (For example, "Lord, thank You for Your Word that says...")

_____

_____

_____

_____

Read John 15:7 and underline it in your Bible. What does God require of you, and what will He do for you?

_____

_____

_____

_____

Say the Scripture and pray the prayer out loud in "Read God's Word Daily Until You Feel Relief from Fear." Add whatever else God has put on your heart to pray. Jot it below to remind you.

_____

_____

_____

6. Read number 8, "Thank God for What He Has Done for You," on page 136 in the book. Then read the following Scriptures and underline them in your Bible. Beneath each one, write down what they tell you about thanking God.

James 1:17

_____

_____

_____

1 Thessalonians 5:16-18

_____

_____

_____

Psalm 50:14-15

_____

_____

_____

Psalm 100:4

_____

_____

_____

Write out a prayer thanking God for all the things you can think of that He has done for you.

_____

_____

_____

_____

Say the Scripture and pray the prayer out loud in "Thank God for What He Has Done for You." Add whatever else God has put on your heart to pray. Jot it below to remind you.

_____

_____

_____

Read number 17, "Tell Someone What God Has Done for You," on pages 142-143 in the book. Then read the following Scriptures and underline them in your Bible. What do they say to you about telling others what God has done for you?

1 Peter 3:15

_____

_____

_____

Psalm 64:9

_____

_____

_____

1 Samuel 12:34

_____

_____

_____

Write out a prayer asking God to help you tell others about what God has done for you. Ask Him to show you whose heart is open to hearing what you want to share.

_____

_____

_____

Say the Scripture and pray the prayer out loud in "Tell Someone What God Has Done for You." Add whatever else God has put on your heart to pray. Jot it below to remind you.

_____

_____

_____

7. Read number 11, "Refuse to Do Anything That Will Compromise Your Walk with God," on pages 137-138 in the book. Then read Psalm 139:23-24 and underline these verses in your Bible. Write out a prayer asking God to show you anything or anyone in your life that compromises your walk with Him. Ask God to help you separate yourself from both.

_____

_____

_____

_____

_____

Read Deuteronomy 7:26 and underline it in your Bible. Other words for "abomination" are "a detestable thing." When you think about having something in your life that is detestable or an abomination to God, it makes you want to get rid of it as quickly as possible. Write out a prayer asking God to show you anything in your house or in your life that is not pleasing to Him so that you can get rid of it. He will bring those things or people to mind.

_____

_____

_____

_____

Say the Scripture and pray the prayer out loud in "Refuse to Do Anything That Will Compromise Your Walk with God." Add whatever else God has put on your heart to pray. Jot it below to remind you.

_____

_____

_____

Read section 15, "Celebrate the Lord's Supper in Remembrance of Him," on pages 141-142 in the book. Then read 1 Corinthians 11:23-26 and underline these verses in your Bible. Jesus commanded us to celebrate the last supper so we would always remember what He accomplished on the cross for us. This is very important, but it's often neglected by people and even some churches. *Not* observing this command of Jesus will compromise your walk with the Lord.

Read 1 Corinthians 11:28-30. These verses give more guidelines about not taking this lightly and not giving the full value and worth to what Jesus did on the cross. We could be suffering with weakness or sickness, even leading to premature death because of minimizing what Jesus did. Write out a prayer asking God to help you understand how to honor Him by celebrating all He did for you.

_____

_____

_____

_____

_____

Say the Scripture and pray the prayer out loud in "Celebrate the Lord's Supper in Remembrance of Him." Add whatever else God has put on your heart to pray. Jot it below to remind you.

_____

_____

_____

8. Read number 12, "Pray and Don't Give Up," on page 138 in the book. Praying about everything that causes you to have fear, standing on the Word of God, and praising and worshiping God are the three most important things you can do to find peace instead of fear.

    Read Luke 18:1-8 in your Bible and underline key verses. If a judge who didn't fear God or regard people would respond to someone who sought his help constantly, how will God respond to someone who prays to Him constantly? Write out your answer as a prayer, asking God to help you not lose heart and give up praying. (For example, "Lord, Your Word encourages me to keep praying and asking You for...")

_____

_____

_____

_____

Read Colossians 4:2 and underline it in your Bible. Write out a prayer asking God to help you do what this verse requires of you. Be especially specific with regard to the pressing things that are causing you to have fear right now.

_____

_____

_____

_____

Say the Scripture and pray the prayer out loud in "Pray and Don't Give Up." Add whatever else God has put on your heart to pray. Jot it below to remind you.

_____

_____

_____

Read number 13, "Pray the Prayer Jesus Taught His Disciples," on pages 139-140 in the book. What connection did the disciples of Jesus make with the prayers of Jesus?

_____

_____

_____

_____

Read Matthew 6:5-8 and underline these verses in your Bible. What did Jesus say about praying?

_____

_____

_____

_____

Read Matthew 6:8-13 and underline verses 9-13 in your Bible. This prayer should be spoken many times so you have it memorized. If you already have it memorized, write it out below from memory. If you have not memorized it yet, write it out below because that will help you remember it. Pray this prayer often because it's the model prayer given to us by Jesus that covers everything you need.

_____

_____

_____

_____

_____

_____

In light of verse 8, why do you think you must ask God for the things He already knows you need? Keep in mind that God wants you to walk with Him daily and come to Him for everything. Write out a prayer asking God to show you anything you are not praying about that you need to bring to Him. As He brings things to mind, include them in this prayer.

_____

_____

_____

_____

_____

Say the Scripture and pray the prayer out loud in "Pray the Prayer Jesus Taught His Disciples." Add whatever else God has put on your heart to pray. Jot it below to remind you.

_____

_____

_____

9. Read number 14, "Ask God to Help You Show Love to Others," on pages 140-141 in the book. Then read the following verses and underline them in your Bible. What do they say about loving others?

Mark 12:30-31

_____

_____

_____

Ephesians 5:1-2

_____

_____

_____

John 15:12-13

_____

_____

_____

1 John 2:11

_____

_____

_____

Hebrews 10:24

_____

_____

_____

Hebrews 13:1

_____

_____

_____

1 Peter 3:8

_____

_____

_____

Romans 13:8-10

_____

_____

_____

_____

_____

Read 1 Corinthians 13:1-4 and underline these verses in your Bible. What do they say about loving others?

_____

_____

_____

_____

_____

_____

_____

Read Romans 12:10-13 and underline these verses in your Bible. Write out a prayer asking God to help you do what is required of you.

_____

_____

_____

_____

_____

Read Matthew 22:36-40 and underline these verses in your Bible. What are the two greatest commandments? Write out your answer as a prayer asking God to help you do those two things.

_____

_____

_____

_____

Say the Scripture and pray the prayer out loud in "Ask God to Help You Show Love to Others." Add whatever else God has put on your heart to pray. Jot it below to remind you.

_____

_____

_____

Read number 19, "Choose to Not Sit in Judgment of Others," on pages 144-145 in the book. Then read Luke 6:37-42 and underline key verses in your Bible. What does this passage of Scripture tell you about why we shouldn't judge others? What happens when we forgive instead?

_____

_____

_____

_____

_____

Write out a prayer asking God to show you every person you are ongoingly critical of and ask Him to help you be released from any kind of a judgmental attitude.

_____

_____

_____

_____

Say the Scripture and pray the prayer out loud in "Choose to Not Sit in Judgment of Others." Add whatever else God has put on your heart to pray. Jot it below to remind you.

_____

_____

_____

10. Read number 16, "Ask God to Reveal His Will for Your Life," on page 142 in the book. Then read Matthew 26:39 and underline it in your Bible. What did Jesus say to His heavenly Father? Do you say that to God?

_____

_____

_____

Read 1 Thessalonians 5:17 again. What is God's will for you? Do you feel you do that? Or do you need to pray more?

_____

_____

_____

Read John 9:31 and underline it in your Bible. What is a great benefit of worshipping God and doing His will?

_____

_____

Write out a prayer asking God to reveal to you what His will is for your life. Include everything you have specific questions about. (For example, where you work, what church you attend, what you do, whom you spend time with, decisions you need to make, etc.)

_____

_____

_____

_____

_____

Say the Scripture and pray the prayer out loud in "Ask God to Reveal His Will for Your Life." Add whatever else God has put on your heart to pray. Jot it below to remind you.

_____

_____

_____

Read number 20, "Give to God and Others So You Store Up Treasures in Heaven," on pages 145-146 in the book. A big part of God's will is giving to Him and giving to others.

Read the following Scriptures and underline them in your Bible. Beneath each one, write what the verse says to you about giving.

Proverbs 22:9

_____

_____

_____

Proverbs 1:19

_____

_____

_____

Psalm 41:1

_____

_____

_____

Read Matthew 6:21 and underline it in your Bible. Write out a prayer asking God to help your heart to always be in the right place so that you treasure what is most important.

_____

_____

_____

_____

_____

Say the Scripture and pray the prayer out loud in "Give to God and Others So You Store Up Treasures in Heaven." Add whatever else God has put on your heart to pray. Jot it below to remind you.

_____

_____

_____

Pray the prayer at the end of chapter 7 on page 147. Add whatever else God puts on your heart. Jot it below.

_____

_____

_____

_____

_____

WEEK EIGHT

Read Chapter 8: "What Are the Enemy's Fear Tactics?"
in *The Power of Praying Through Fear*

1. Read Psalm 64:1-2 and underline these verses in your Bible. What did David specifically ask God to do for him?

_____

_____

_____

Read John 10:10 and underline it in your Bible. What does our enemy come to do?

_____

_____

_____

What did Jesus come to earth to do?

_____

_____

_____

What has the enemy stolen from you? What has he killed or destroyed in your life? If you don't know, write out a prayer asking God to show you.

_____

_____

_____

_____

Read the following Scriptures and underline them in your Bible. Beneath each one, write down why you do not need to fear evil.

Psalm 23:4

_____

_____

_____

Deuteronomy 3:22

_____

_____

_____

2. Read 1 Peter 5:8 and underline it in your Bible. Why do we have to be vigilant in prayer?

_____

_____

_____

Do you feel the enemy has devoured some things in your life? What are they? If you are not sure, write out a prayer asking God to show you where the enemy has done that. (For example, finances, relationships, health, etc.) Ask God to help you be vigilant to pray so the enemy cannot take what is yours.

_____

_____

_____

_____

Read John 8:44 and underline it in your Bible. What did Jesus say about the enemy of our soul?

_____

_____

_____

_____

Can you identify any lie of the enemy you have accepted as truth about yourself or your situation in the past? If so, explain. If you're not sure, ask God to show you that. Either way, write out your answer in a prayer asking God to keep you from being deceived by the enemy.

_____

_____

_____

_____

Do you know of anyone close to you who is believing a lie or being deceived by the enemy? If so, write out a prayer for that person asking God to lift the blinders off of them so they can see the truth. If you can't think of anyone like that, write out a prayer for someone you are especially concerned about that they not become deceived or misled by the lies of the enemy.

_____

_____

_____

_____

Read Romans 8:1 and underline it in your Bible. What is true about those of us who receive Jesus?

_____

_____

This means you do not have to feel condemnation from the past, because Jesus paid the price for your sins. If you have done something that is not pleasing to God since you received Jesus and you feel guilty, take it to the Lord in repentance and confession so He can free you from it. Guilt weakens you, and it's a burden too heavy for you to carry. Write out a prayer asking God to show you any place in your mind or soul that is carrying guilt of some kind. If you know what it is, confess it before God and ask to be liberated from it. If you don't know what is causing you to feel condemnation, ask God to reveal it to you so you can be free of it. Ask God to show you if you have been listening to the lies of the enemy saying you are condemned.

_____

_____

_____

_____

_____

Read Isaiah 54:14 and underline it in your Bible. What does this verse say is true of those who have chosen to live God's way and serve Him?

_____

_____

_____

3. Read Ephesians 6:12 and underline it in your Bible. What does this verse tell you about who we struggle with in our spiritual war?

_____

_____

_____

_____

Read Matthew 11:28-30 and underline these verses in your Bible. How can you find rest even in times of enemy attack? Write out your answer as a prayer asking God to help you find that place of rest in your life. (For example, "Lord, I come to You feeling burdened by...")

_____

_____

_____

_____

Read the following Scriptures and underline them in your Bible. Below each one, answer the question, *What do you need to do to resist evil?* Write out your answer as a prayer asking God to help you do that. (For example, "Lord, give me the wisdom and understanding I need to be able to...")

1 Thessalonians 5:19-22

_____

_____

_____

Romans 12:9

_____

_____

_____

Proverbs 3:31

_____

_____

_____

Read 1 Corinthians 3:11 and Luke 6:47-48 and underline these verses in your Bible. What do you need to do in order to have a solid foundation from which you cannot be shaken?

_____

_____

_____

_____

4. Read the following Scriptures and underline them in your Bible. Answer the question below each one.

    Romans 8:9. How can we live in the Spirit? Tell what happens if we don't?

    _____

    _____

    _____

    Ephesians 1:13-14. What does it mean to be sealed with the Holy Spirit of Promise?

    _____

    _____

    _____

    1 Corinthians 1:18. What is the message of the cross to unbelievers, and what is it to us who believe?

    _____

    _____

    _____

    Read 2 Corinthians 13:3-5 and underline these verses in your Bible. Jesus lives in you because you have received Him, and by doing so you have become a sanctified vessel in which the Holy Spirit of God—also called the Spirit of Christ—can now dwell. Jesus was resurrected by the power of God, and we will live with Him for eternity by the power of the Holy Spirit in us. You cannot be disqualified from that promise unless you specifically reject the Holy Spirit of God and decide to live with the enemy on the dark side. No one who has the Holy Spirit within them—whom you have if you've received Jesus—would ever reject Him. In light of this passage of Scripture, what is true of you and your relationship with Jesus? What are you supposed to do?

_____

_____

_____

_____

_____

_____

Read the following Scriptures and underline them in your Bible. What do these verses tell you about the holiness of God?

1 Samuel 2:2

_____

_____

_____

Revelation 15:4

_____

_____

_____

Read Luke 1:74-75 and underline these verses in your Bible. They are from a prophecy given by Zacharias—the new father of a baby who would one day be John the Baptist. By the power of the Holy Spirit, Zacharias foretold of the coming Messiah and what He would do for us. In light of this passage of Scripture, write out a prayer thanking God for what our Messiah, Jesus, came to earth to do for us. Ask God to help you do what He wants you to do for *Him*.

_____

_____

_____

_____

_____

5. Read Romans 16:19-20 and underline these verses in your Bible. They mean that we don't have to be an expert in what the acts of evil are. But in what way are we to be wise? What will God do for us? Write out your answers as a prayer below, asking God to help you do those things. Thank God for what the last verse promises He will do for you.

_____

_____

_____

_____

_____

Read Colossians 2:13-15 and underline these verses in your Bible. What did Jesus accomplish for us on the cross?

_____

_____

_____

_____

_____

Read 2 Chronicles 20:15-18 and underline key verses in your Bible. When facing a formidable enemy, what was King Jehoshaphat told to do by God? (verses 15-17)

_____

_____

_____

_____

What was King Jehoshaphat's response to this word from God?

_____

_____

_____

When we walk with God and depend on Him, He fights our battles for us when the enemy attacks. But it doesn't happen automatically without any input from us. We have to be completely submitted to God, living His way, and being certain that we are where God wants us to be and doing what He wants us to do. That takes much prayer and seeking God's will on a daily basis. It's difficult to wade through all the voices telling you what to do. You have to be able to *hear* God's voice to your heart, from His Word, and by spending time with Him in prayer. Also, godly and wise counsel is important. Write out a prayer thanking God that when you face an onslaught of the enemy that puts the odds against you, if you will pray, believe His Word, and worship Him, God will rise up and strike the enemy down.

_____

_____

_____

_____

_____

6. Read John 14:12-14 and 1 Corinthians 12:3 and underline these verses in your Bible. You have authority in prayer because Jesus has given you authority to pray in His name. The Holy Spirit in you is also the proof of your authority in prayer. Write out a prayer thanking God for the authority He has given you. Ask Him to help you pray with the authority He has given you over the enemy. Ask Him to teach you the full significance of Him giving you the authority to pray in His name.

_____

_____

_____

_____

Read Colossians 1:13-14 and underline these verses in your Bible. Write them out as a declaration about yourself. (For example, "Jesus has delivered me from...")

_____

_____

_____

_____

7. Read the following verses and underline them in your Bible. Under each one, write what you are to do with regard to evil.

    Romans 12:21

    _____

    _____

    _____

    1 Timothy 4:1-2

    _____

    _____

    _____

Read the following Scriptures and underline them in your Bible. Below each one, write down how you can be saved from your enemies. What will the Lord do?

Psalm 18:2-3

_____

_____

_____

Psalm 18:16-19

_____

_____

_____

Psalm 18:28-30

_____

_____

_____

Read Hebrews 4:12 and underline it in your Bible. What is our most important weapon against the temptation to drift away from the truth? Why?

_____

_____

_____

_____

Read 1 Corinthians 10:12-13 and underline these verses in your Bible. What do they say to people who are tempted beyond what they feel they can handle?

_____

_____

_____

_____

8. Read James 4:7 and underline it in your Bible. How do you resist the devil? What happens when you do that?

_____

_____

Read Isaiah 59:19 and underline it in your Bible. What does God do for those who fear Him?

_____

_____

_____

_____

Read the following Scriptures and underline them in your Bible. In light of these verses, how do we resist the enemy?

Ephesians 5:8-11

_____

_____

_____

Psalm 84:1-2

_____

_____

_____

9. Read Ephesians 6:10-18 and underline these verses in your
    Bible—or underline the words and phrases most important to
    you. Answer the following questions.

    Where are we supposed to find our strength? (verse 10)

    _____

    _____

    _____

    What are we supposed to put on and why? (verses 11-13)

    _____

    _____

    _____

    What are we supposed to put on to protect us? (verses 14-15)

    _____

    _____

    _____

What are our weapons of warfare? (verses 16-17)

_____

_____

_____

What are we to do in an ongoing manner? (verse 18)

_____

_____

_____

Read 2 Corinthians 3:17 and underline it in your Bible. In light of this verse, what should we always seek when we are afraid? Write out your answer as a prayer asking God to help you remember to do that at the first sign of an enemy attack.

_____

_____

_____

_____

Read Psalm 27:1-3 and underline verses 2 and 3 in your Bible. What did David say about fear?

_____

_____

_____

_____

10. Pray the prayer on pages 172-173 in the book. Include anything else God puts on your heart to pray. Jot it down below to remind you.

_____

_____

_____

_____

_____

WEEK NINE

Read Chapter 9: "What Overcomes the Fear of Death?"
in *The Power of Praying Through Fear*

1. Read 2 Corinthians 5:1-8 and underline key verses in your Bible. The apostle Paul refers to our earthly body as a tent, but when we die we will trade our tent for a building from God. The tent is temporary. The building from God is eternal. The guarantee of all this being a smooth transition is the Holy Spirit in us. This means there is no time lapse between dying and being in the presence of Jesus. It is instantaneous. How do you feel about your own death? Does it worry or frighten you? Do you have peace about it? Does it give you peace to know there is an instant transfer from your earthly body to your heavenly body, and you are instantly transported into the presence of Jesus as well? Write out your answers to these questions as a prayer telling God what you fear about dying and what you find comforting in these verses.

---

2. Read 2 Corinthians 4:16-18 and underline these verses in your Bible. Even though our body is aging and will be dying at some point, what is true of our inner self?

_____

_____

_____

Even when we suffer here on earth, it's temporary compared to eternity with the Lord. Write out a prayer asking God to help you understand that the things you see and experience are temporary compared with that which we do not see, which is eternal. Ask God to give you the right perspective on going to be with Him at the end of your life.

_____

_____

_____

_____

_____

Read John 8:51 and underline it in your Bible. This means we will not experience death the way others who do not live for the Lord will experience it. Write out a prayer telling God what concerns you most about your death. Ask Him to give you total peace about it so that it's not a source of fear for you. Don't be afraid to think or write about dying. It doesn't mean you will be dying soon. It means you can settle the issue in your mind and heart so that you don't have to live in fear of it.

_____

_____

_____

_____

_____

3. Read Luke 10:19-20 and underline these verses in your Bible. Even though Jesus has given us authority over all the power of the enemy, our greatest cause for rejoicing is that we have received Jesus and our names are written in heaven. Write out a prayer thanking God for that.

    _____

    _____

    _____

    _____

    Read Revelation 20:12,15; 21:27; and Daniel 12:1 and underline these verses in your Bible. How important is it to have your name written in the Lamb's Book of Life?

    _____

    _____

    _____

    _____

4. Read John 16:33 and underline it in your Bible. What encouragement do these words of Jesus give you?

    _____

    _____

    _____

Read Revelation 1:18 and underline it in your Bible. What do these words of Jesus say about all He accomplished on the cross for you?

_____

_____

Read Hebrews 12:2 and underline it in your Bible. What is Jesus described as being to us?

_____

_____

Why did Jesus endure the cross?

_____

_____

Where is Jesus now?

_____

_____

Read John 11:25-27 and underline these verses in your Bible. Do you believe what Jesus said is true for you? Write out your answer in a prayer telling God what you believe in these verses. (For example, "Lord, I believe You are...")

_____

_____

_____

_____

Read Hebrews 2:14-15 and underline these verses in your Bible. What did Jesus accomplish for you in His death and resurrection?

_____

_____

_____

_____

5. Read Psalm 51:10 and underline it in your Bible. Write out this verse from a psalm of David as a prayer asking God to give you a heart and spirit that stands strong in His truth and His ways. Ask Him to help you have the right attitude. Pray this prayer whenever you feel your heart is not right.

_____

_____

_____

_____

Ask God to show you any wrong attitudes or thoughts you might have that you need to get rid of because they are not pleasing to Him and do not glorify Him.

_____

_____

_____

_____

Read John 14:27 and underline it in your Bible. Jesus told us that we cannot enjoy the peace He gives us if we refuse to let go of the things that trouble us and cause us to be fearful. Write out a prayer to God telling Him whatever troubles your heart right now. Don't hesitate. No one has to know or read this. We all have things that trouble us and need to bring them before God. Tell Him how you would like Him to answer this prayer.

_____

_____

_____

_____

6. Read the following Scriptures and underline them in your Bible. Beneath each one, write out what they tell you about dying and where we go afterward. What comfort does each one give you?

Revelation 14:13

_____

_____

_____

Hebrews 2:14-15

_____

_____

_____

Revelation 2:10

_____

_____

_____

Revelation 21:1-4

_____

_____

_____

7. Read Psalm 116:15 and underline it in your Bible. Write out a prayer thanking God that your death is precious to Him. Ask Him to protect you from anything happening to you before the day and hour that is His perfect will for you to go and be with Him.

_____

_____

_____

_____

Write out a prayer asking God to help you communicate to people that you know where you are going when you die. You must be absolutely sure in order to convince others. If you have any doubt, ask God to give you the assurance you need.

_____

_____

_____

_____

Write out a prayer asking God to help you be prepared for being in heaven with Him. That includes not leaving a mess on earth for your family or bad feelings between you and anyone. Ask Him to show you anything you need to take care of here. (For example, having a will, paying off debt, finding out what possessions you have that people want, getting right with God and others, etc.) Doing all this doesn't mean you are dying soon. It means you will have more peace about the future.

_____

_____

_____

_____

Read Psalm 39:4-7 and underline key verses in your Bible. If David asked God about how his life would end, so can we. Write out a prayer asking God for the same things David did. Ask Him to remind you that your hope is always in Him.

_____

_____

_____

_____

Read John 14:13. How does this verse comfort you with regard to dying?

_____

_____

_____

_____

8. How do you feel about the end-times? Are you fearful or troubled about what is to come? Do you avoid thinking about it? Or are you joyful because it means Jesus is returning soon—especially as we see so many signs of the end-times mentioned in the book of Revelation? Do you need to know more? Describe below what you believe or feel about the tumultuous days described before Jesus' return.

_____

_____

_____

_____

_____

_____

If you have time, read all of Psalm 73 and underline the parts of it you want to especially remember. It's a great psalm because many of us have the same thoughts the psalmist had about ungodly and evil people who always succeed and prosper and never seem to suffer. He thought that perhaps he had kept himself pure in heart and obedient to God for nothing. That is, until he "went into the sanctuary of God" and then he "understood their end" (Psalm 73:17). It's very powerful to read the entire psalm, so please do so if you have time now. If not, read Psalm 73:23-26 to find out the psalmist's final conclusion. Write out a prayer of thanksgiving to God for His reward—all that is listed in these four verses—to those who follow Him.

_____

_____

_____

_____

_____

_____

Read the following Scriptures and underline them in your Bible.
Beneath each one, describe the hope in that verse for you.

Romans 8:11

_____

_____

_____

Romans 14:8

_____

_____

_____

John 5:24

_____

_____

_____

Psalm 23:4

_____

_____

_____

2 Timothy 1:12

_____

_____

_____

9. Read the following Scriptures and underline them in your Bible. Below each one, write what comfort they bring to your heart.

Revelation 1:1-3

_____

_____

_____

Revelation 3:10-11

_____

_____

_____

Revelation 3:20-21

_____

_____

_____

Revelation 7:14-17

_____

_____

_____

Revelation 12:10-11

_____

_____

_____

10. Pray the prayer on page 193 in the book. Add any specifics that God puts on your heart to pray about and jot them below so you will remember to pray for them again.

_____

_____

_____

_____

_____

WEEK TEN

Read Chapter 10: "What Can Keep Us from Fearing the Future?"
in *The Power of Praying Through Fear*

1. How do you feel about your future? What about the future of
   your family? What concerns you most?

   _____

   _____

   _____

   _____

   _____

   Read the following Scriptures and underline them in your Bible.
   Below each one, write down what that passage of Scripture
   speaks to you about your future.

   Jeremiah 29:11

   _____

   _____

   _____

Psalm 84:11

_____

_____

_____

Romans 8:31-35

_____

_____

_____

Psalm 16:11

_____

_____

_____

Write out a prayer about your future. Be completely frank about your fears, doubts, or worries. Ask God to give you peace about everything that concerns you.

_____

_____

_____

_____

_____

2. Answer the following questions.

Do you believe Jesus is who He said He is? Why do you believe that?

_____

_____

_____

_____

Do you believe Jesus spoke the truth or He didn't? Why do you believe that?

_____

_____

_____

_____

Do you believe God's Word is true or not? Why do you believe that?

_____

_____

_____

_____

Have you declared your trust in Jesus and received Him? Why or why not?

_____

_____

_____

_____

Do you believe God loves you and hears your prayers? Why or why not?

_____

_____

_____

_____

Do you believe God will answer your prayers in His way and His time? Why or why not?

_____

_____

_____

_____

Do you believe God is powerful enough to keep you and your family safe? Do you trust Him to guide you in that regard? Why or why not?

_____

_____

_____

_____

Read Matthew 6:25 and underline it in your Bible. What does this verse say to you with regard to any fear you may have about the future?

_____

_____

_____

_____

3. Read Psalm 112:1,6-8 and underline these verses in your Bible. They describe the blessings of those who fear the Lord. What do they speak to you about your future?

    _____

    _____

    _____

    _____

    Read Psalm 37:3-8 and underline verses 5-8 in your Bible. What are you supposed to do to ensure a good future?

    _____

    _____

    _____

    _____

    Read Psalm 37:23-26 and underline these verses in your Bible. What is the future like for you when you live God's way?

    _____

    _____

    _____

    _____

Read Psalm 37:37 and underline it in your Bible. What is the future of a person who lives God's way?

_____

_____

_____

Write out a prayer asking God to guide you every day and help you to walk with Him into the future He has for you.

_____

_____

_____

_____

4. What are the five things you need to remember about your future? How do they help you to face it in a hopeful and positive way? (See pages 204-206 in the book.) Make your response personal to you. Write out your first answer as a note to yourself. Write your second answer under each number as a prayer.

   1. I must remember that God's...

   _____

   _____

   _____

   "Lord, help me to remember that...

   _____

   _____

   _____

2. I must remember that God gave me...

_____

_____

_____

"Lord, help me to remember that You gave me...

_____

_____

_____

3. I must remember that God wants me to...

_____

_____

_____

"Lord, help me remember that You want me to...

_____

_____

_____

4. I must remember that when I make plans for my future, I should not...

_____

_____

_____

"Lord, help me to always remember that when I make plans for the future to...

_____

_____

_____

5. I must remember that God is...

_____

_____

_____

"Lord, help me to remember that even when I am overwhelmed by the future, You are...

_____

_____

_____

5. What do you picture as a good future for you and your family? Write out your answer as a prayer asking God for that. Ask Him to show you if what you want lines up with His will for your life.

_____

_____

_____

_____

_____

Write out a prayer asking God to help you walk closely to Him every day so that you will always be where He wants you to be, doing what He wants you to do.

_____

_____

_____

_____

_____

6. Read the following Scriptures and underline them in your Bible. Beneath each one, write what those verses tell you to do with regard to your future.

Psalm 62:5-8

_____

_____

_____

Psalm 63:7-8

_____

_____

_____

Psalm 27:13

_____

_____

_____

Read Deuteronomy 28:7-8 and underline these verses in your Bible. What will God do for you when the enemy attacks?

_____

_____

_____

_____

Do you ever find that you are receiving a lot of advice from people who do not have godly wisdom? Are predictions being made about your future from sources who do not rely on input from God or His Word? Explain.

_____

_____

_____

_____

Write out a prayer asking God to show you where you are receiving input about your future that is not from Him.

_____

_____

_____

_____

7. Read the following Scriptures and underline them in your Bible. What comfort do these verses bring to you regarding your future?

Romans 8:38-39

_____

_____

_____

1 Corinthians 15:58

_____

_____

_____

Matthew 5:5-11

_____

_____

_____

1 Thessalonians 5:23

_____

_____

_____

Psalm 27:13

_____

_____

_____

8. Read Hebrews 12:1-2 and underline these verses in your Bible. What are you supposed to do with your life?

_____

_____

_____

_____

Read the following Scriptures and underline them in your Bible. What are you supposed to do and what will happen when you do it?

Isaiah 40:31

_____

_____

_____

2 Timothy 4:7

_____

_____

_____

Romans 8:37

_____

_____

_____

Philippians 3:13-14

_____

_____

_____

Psalm 131:2

_____

_____

_____

9. Read the following Scriptures and underline them in your Bible. Write down what each one says about your future and what you should do.

Psalm 118:24

_____

_____

_____

Proverbs 23:18

_____

_____

_____

James 5:8

_____

_____

_____

2 Corinthians 3:18

_____

_____

_____

Romans 15:13

_____

_____

_____

Psalm 33:20

_____

_____

_____

10. Pray the prayer on page 215 in the book. Below write down other specifics that God brings to mind for you to pray about so you will remember to pray for them again.

_____

_____

_____

_____

_____

Answers to Prayer

*What answers to prayer have you seen since
you started praying through fear? Be sure to
write them down. It's important to acknowledge
what God has done and praise Him for it.*

_____

_____

_____

_____

_____

_____

_____

_____

_____

_____

_____

_____

_____

_____

_____

Answers to Prayer

Answers to Prayer

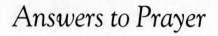

Answers to Prayer

Answers to Prayer

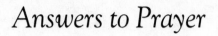

Answers to Prayer

Is Fear Affecting Your Life?
Does It Ever Steal Your Peace and Disturb Your Sleep?

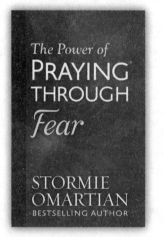

In today's world, fear has become epidemic. It takes away our sense of well-being; stresses our mind, body, and soul; and can keep us from doing what we need to do.

The good news is that you can enjoy freedom from damaging fear by establishing your heart and mind on the comforting truths of God and learning how to pray in power. Stormie Omartian shows you what to *think*, *say*, and *pray* the moment you sense fear in your heart, and what you can *do* to combat anxiety. She offers help for overcoming such life-inhibiting fears as:

- fear of rejection
- fear of evil
- fear of suffering
- fear of death
- fear of loss
- fear of the future

As you rely on the Lord's strength to conquer fear, you will discover the distinction between the fear God *does not want* us to have, the fear God *allows* us to have, and the fear God *wants* us to have. Learn to pray and claim the power, love, and sound mind God has for you.

To learn more about Harvest House books and
to read sample chapters, visit our website:

www.harvesthousepublishers.com

HARVEST HOUSE PUBLISHERS
EUGENE, OREGON